CHINA DECORATION

BY

KATHLEEN MANN

AUTHOR OF 'APPLIQUÉ DESIGN AND METHOD'
'EMBROIDERY DESIGN,' 'DESIGN FROM PEASANT ART,' ETC.

WITH COLOUR FRONTISPIECE
SIX PLATES FROM PHOTOGRAPHS
AND MANY LINE DRAWINGS
BY THE AUTHOR

PITMAN PUBLISHING CORPORATION
NEW YORK · TORONTO · LONDON

FIRST PUBLISHED IN U.S.A. 1953

MADE IN GREAT BRITAIN
PRINTED BY MORRISON AND GIBB LTD., LONDON AND EDINBURGH

PREFACE

THIS book has been written at a time when there is a strong revival in the craft of hand-decorated china. It is written not only for teachers and art students but for the housewife and any others who may be interested in a craft which may be practised at home. I hope that the many people who write to me from all over the country (some from as far as Shetland) will find their questions answered here.

As a means of self-expression, as a means of producing something beautiful—or at least good to look at—and as an escape from the monotony of routine duties, china decoration is an ideal occupation. But it is important that the present revived enthusiasm for an old craft should be led and guided towards a high standard of design.

While we may appreciate the china and porcelain painted in the late eighteenth century, when anything from an elaborate landscape to a portrait was used as a subject for decoration. it is unlikely that with the changed conditions of to-day anyone would have the time or inclination to work in the style of those past artists. Because actual paintings in miniature were painted on china, the name china-painting was appropriate. In recent years this craft has been rather 'looked down upon' by the intellectuals of the design world, which is not to be wondered at, since the attitude of mind of the majority of china-painters has become dull and unimaginative. Many have been satisfied to paint would-be naturalistic flowers on pieces of china, with little or no consideration for the shape, size, and quality of the article to be decorated. This book is purposely called *China Decoration*. Its aim throughout is to lay stress on the importance of good proportion, line, colour, and the feeling for decoration which would be in sympathy with contemporary furniture and interior decoration. It is hoped that readers will gain pleasure from their work, and have reason to feel proud of their achievements.

KATHLEEN MANN

Aberdeen

CONTENTS

1. FIRST PRINCIPLES AND MATERIALS

THE attitude of mind of the would-be china decorator is all important. It would be a pity to start with the intention of copying work which factory and machine methods can produce easily and in great quantities. Rather, the aim should be to bring to the china a very personal touch, and to give the work that element of individuality and surprise so often lacking in the mass-produced article.

Commercial firms have their professional designers and hand-painters. These artists work in collaboration with the business men and salesmen who largely control the design by their knowledge of public taste in this country and abroad. But the amateur has complete freedom to follow his or her fancy, and thus the opportunity to take the lead towards new and original work. If a high æsthetic level were reached in this field it could mean a gradual improvement in the taste of the general public, who would demand only the better-designed ware from the commercial firms, and with a lack of demand, it is possible that the more commonplace and vulgar designs would disappear.

The need for patience and practice in the initial stages must be stressed ; many beginners are inclined to ' run before they can walk.' It is good to remember that a simple design well considered will always have more dignity and beauty than an elaborate one which is ill considered and poorly executed. To begin with, the use of designs drawn on paper should be avoided, for it is difficult to obtain on a paper surface the feeling of a three-dimensional object with a smooth glazed surface.

To avoid waste of materials, it is sometimes a good plan to experiment with poster colours, or water-colour, to which a little soap or paste has been added. In this way it is possible to plan the decoration on the object itself, wiping off and starting again, until satisfied that the best possible proportion and placing has been achieved, and only then proceeding to work in on-glaze colours.

The following is a list of requirements. Although it appears rather formidable, it should be noted that only those marked * are necessary for the beginner.

There is a large range of camel-hair brushes especially made for china decorating. This drawing illustrates a few of them. Each differently shaped brush is made in sizes ranging from small to large.

---

    * A selection of six or eight colours (see list opposite).
    * Flux (assists in fusing the colour—not absolutely essential).
    * Grounding oil.
    * Fat oil of turpentine.
    * Pure turpentine.
    * Substitute turpentine.
      Oil of cloves.
      Oil of lavender.
      Alcohol.
    * Cotton rags (not fluffy).
    * Pieces of old silk.
    * Animal wool.
      Sellotape.
      Plasticine.
    * Palette knife.
      Bone or ivory spatula.
    * Glass palette (unground on one side).
      Glass mullet.
      Banding wheel.
    * Selection of brushes (see diagram above).

8

Sometimes it is necessary to improvise, and the following suggestions may be useful.

For alcohol—methylated spirits.
For animal wool—cotton wool.
Palette knife—old table knife.
Bone or ivory spatula—plastic egg-spoon with flat handle.
Glass palette—piece of glass rubbed down with fine carborundum powder and water.
Banding Wheel—Cake icing disc, or a gramophone fitted with a circular piece of wood with a central hole to bring the disc level with the top of the central pin. One with a fixed arm and sound box will not do.

Proper care of materials can save time and money. If brushes and palette are left dirty for any length of time they are difficult to clean and the brushes will wear out more quickly than they should. Palette, brushes, mullet, knives, etc., should be cleaned with alcohol, methylated spirit, or substitute turpentine, and then be thoroughly washed with warm water and soap, rinsed, and left to dry.

Powder colours may be kept conveniently in glass tubes, or small bottles ; the colour can then be seen at a glance instead of hunting through paper packets. Some colours appear very similar before firing, and therefore the bottles should be labelled so that no mistake is made when refilling.

Enamel on-glaze colours in powder form :

Cherry	Lilac	Turquoise Sky
Flame	Mauve	Lemon Yellow
Poppy	Hyacinth	Citron Yellow
Indian Red	Puce	Silver Yellow
Asiatic Red	Salmon	Straw Yellow
Scarlet	Flesh	Marigold Yellow
Blood Red	Forget-me-not Blue	Amber
Rubis d'or	Lining Blue	Orange
Purple Blackberry	Superior Blue	Alexander Orange
Purple Crimson	Lapis Blue	Nelson Orange
Purple Strawberry	Paris Blue	Tangerine Orange
Violet Red	Cobalt Blue	Cora Yellow
Violet Rhine	Delphinium Blue	Coral Red
Carmine	Glorious Blue	Celadon Green
Pale Pink	Mazarine Blue	Palisy Green
Philadelphia Pink	Turquoise Celeste	Cucumber Green
Rose du Barry	Turquoise Electric	River Green

Mermaid Green	Paradise Green	Purple Brown
Peacock Green	Moorland Green	Paris Brown
Water Green	Crest Green	Romany Brown
Fern Green	Maize Brown	Buff
Smilax Green	Border Brown	Pearl Grey
Olive Green	Velasquez Brown	Silver Grey
Gordon Green	Brunswick Brown	Fruit Grey
Golden Elder Green	Wood Brown	Paris Black
May Green	Hazel Brown	Intense Black
Dutch Green	French Brown	Spanish Black

The above is not a complete list of powder on-glaze colours, but is sufficient to indicate how extensive is the range. There are several firms producing colours for china decoration. It will be found that colours and their names vary with each manufacturer.

Colours can also be obtained in tube form; a French firm supplies colours of excellent quality. Because of the heavy government tax these colours seem expensive compared to the powder colours. They are, however, more economical to use when small areas are to be covered. All that is needed as a medium is a little turpentine. There are occasions when the addition of a little clove oil will prevent too quick drying, and sometimes a little extra fat oil may be an advantage (read page 12, paragraph 3, and page 26, paragraph 1).

Tube colours (Lacroix), over glaze :

Bleu céleste
  ciel azur
  ciel clair
  Delft
  foncé
  Indien
  lavande
  old blue
  ordinaire
  outremer riche
  riche
  Victoria
  vieux Rouen
Bluet
Bouton d'or
Brun n°3 bitume
  n°4 foncé ou 17
Brun clair
  foncé
  giroflée
  jaune
  loutre
  M ou 108
  marron
  mordoré
  noir

Brun rouge riche
  sépia
  Van Dyck
Café au lait
Carmélite
Carmin tendre A
  tendre n°1
  n°2
  n°3 foncé
Céladon
Chamois
Corail
Fondant général
Gris n°1 ou tendre
  n°2
  n°6 perie
Gris d'acier
  noir
  roux
  tourterelle
Isabelle
Jaune d'argent
  chinois
  fixe
Jaune d'ivoire (47 de Sèvres)

jonquille
  à meler (41 de Sèvres)
  orange
  d'aurane
Laque carminée
Lilas fusible
Mais
Mauve
Noir corbeau
Noir d'ivoire
Ocre
  foncé
Pourpre n°2
  cramoisi
  riche
  rubis
Relief blanc chinois
  blanc fixe
  jaune pour or
Rose Bengale
  de Chine
  fuxible
  Japon
  Pompadour
Rouge brilliant
  capucine

10

chair n°1	n°7 noir	lumière
chair n°2	n°36 T	mousse J
chair foncé	bleu riche	mousse V
Rouge égyptien	bronze	olive
laqueux	canard	pomme
orangé	chrome 3 B	russe
Saumon	chrome riche	de vessie
Torquoise bleu	d'eau au chrome	Violet de fer
verte riche	d'eau au cuivre	de fer, teinte grise
Vert n°5 pré	émeraude	d'or clair
n°6 brun	pour fonds	d'or foncé

From time to time new paints and mediums for decorating china appear on the market. Some of these may be useful in schools and for occupational therapy, when time and cost may make the real craft of china decoration impossible ; they could find a place in helping pupils towards a sense of design and, in the case of occupational therapy, give the patients pleasure and a certain amount of exercise and hand-control.

There are of course no colours or mediums which can take the place in appearance and durability of real on-glaze colours which fire into the glaze. In comparison any other mediums have a " surfacy " and varnished appearance. However, a preparation recently introduced is more durable than most ; it is coated over designs painted in a special paint and baked in the home oven at 350°F (117°C).

2. COLOUR PREPARATIONS AND BRUSH PRACTICE

IT is inadvisable to decorate china which has been used, for old china is apt to throw off impurities when fired, and these cause little greenish and grey blotches to appear.

The china should be very thoroughly cleaned before commencing work. It should be rubbed over with a little turpentine, or better still with a few drops of pure alcohol. Turpentine cleans it well, but is inclined to leave the surface a little sticky, and small hairs and specks of dust may settle on it. When the china has been thoroughly prepared, it should be put in some dust-proof box or cupboard until the colours are mixed, and everything is ready for work to start.

Because each colour seems to have a character of its own, only approximate proportions can be given. It will soon be judged when a little more or less oil is desirable. China which has a thick and very glossy glaze needs a little more fat to make the colour adhere than does a thinner more matt glaze such as is often found on earthenware pieces. A good proportion to start with is :

3 parts colour (say small teaspoonfuls).
1 part flux.
6 drops fat oil.
Turpentine to mix.

Place the colour and flux on the palette, add some turpentine. With the glass mullet, or with a palette knife, grind the colour well until all feeling of grit disappears ; the fat oil can be added either before or after grinding. If yellows are being used, the colours should not be ground with a metal knife ; failing a glass mullet, an ivory, bone or plastic spatula should be used. Metal is inclined to change the colour of the yellow range.

With a medium-sized brush, and then with the finest possible brush, considerable time should be spent in line practice—thick, thin, straight, wavy and crossed lines ; lines which start thick and end in a hair stroke ; and ones which start fine and broaden out

12

This illustration shows the type of lines which are useful in china decoration. Similar lines should be practised until they can be done with ease. It should be noted how the lower groups of lines suggest growth, lines flowing from each other. This form of line practice is useful as a basis for leaf or floral designs.

Zigzags, waves and lines which cross each other (cross hatching) can form designs for china decoration, either by themselves or in conjunction with other motifs.

The character of brush strokes when the brush is placed firmly **on** to the china and gradually lifted or when it is placed down gradually and the pressure increased just before it is lifted should be noted. The drawings above illustrate these points, although it is impossible in a line-block reproduction to show the slight tonal effect gained by the varied pressure of the brush when using on-glaze colours.

14

Tonal effects can be obtained by using groups of lines. A few thin lines widely spaced will give a lighter effect than lines of the same thickness placed closer together. Darker still will be the effect if the closely placed lines are made thicker. These points are illustrated above, and also the method of graduating tone by starting with lines widely spaced and gradually bringing them closer together.

as the brush is pressed more heavily on the china. Suggested types of lines to practise are illustrated on pages 13, 14 and 15.

When satisfied that the free lines flow pleasantly, control can be achieved by pencilling a line on a plate, or tile, and trying with a steady hand to repeat the line in colour immediately above and below the pencilled line. It is important to realise that some colours need different brush treatment from others. It will be found for example that Indian Red and Black are colours which can be applied with a sweeping stroke of the brush, whereas mauves and pinks need the brush held in an upright position, and moved slowly, so that the colour flows down on to the china. The latter colours, if put on with a sweeping movement, are apt to divide and form a 'railway-line' effect.

Experiments should be made with lines crossing each other, either straight or diagonally (cross hatching) and notice taken how the density of colour is affected by the thickness of the lines and their spacing (page 15).

Designs can be arrived at simply by the use of line work. But although these designs look very simple, it must be remembered that the thickness or 'weight' of a line can make or mar them; likewise, the width between the lines, and the distribution of any group of lines. No rules can be laid down with regard to this thickness and distribution. Some have an instinctive feeling for these points, others have to learn by trial and error. If you are willing to try several arrangements, and are critical of your work, this sense or 'taste' for proportion will gradually develop.

Opposite are a few bold rhythmic lines used to suggest simple flower and leaf shapes. On a fairly large pot such lines and motifs can be used to accentuate the shape of the pot.

Designs which appear very free and simple often require a great deal of thought, consideration and practice in order to obtain a really spontaneous effect. Considerable time should be spent looking at and feeling the shape of the article to be decorated before work is commenced.

3. DIVIDING THE SURFACE

I⊤ is sometimes necessary to divide the rounded surface of a piece of china into a number of equal parts. A quick and satisfactory solution of the problem, and one sufficiently accurate for a hand-decorated article, is the cut-paper method.

If a plate is to have a decorated border, and the design demands that the border should be divided into eight equal parts, the plate should be placed upside down on a piece of fairly thin, smooth paper, and a line drawn round the circumference. The circle is then cut out and folded exactly in half, and placed—still folded—on to the plate, the curve of the paper exactly coinciding with the edge of the plate. A line is then drawn across the plate, using the folded edge of the paper as a guide (page 19, 1). The paper is folded again, and a line drawn, this time at right angles to the previous line, dividing one half of the plate into quarters (2). This line is completed by changing the position of the paper to the other half of the plate, a line once more being drawn where the folded edge of the paper crosses the plate. It is now divided into four sections (3). By folding the paper once more and repeating the process, the plate can be divided into eight parts (4). If only the outer edge of the plate is to be divided the paper circle should be cut just within the drawn line. It should be folded three times, creased well, and opened and laid on to the plate. A small mark should be made where the end of each fold meets the plate (5).

Cups can also be divided into sections by this method. In this case, two circular pieces of paper will require to be cut, one equal in circumference to the top of the cup, and one equal to the base (6). The two circles should be folded into the required number of segments, creased well, and opened out. With one fold of the paper of the larger circle placed pointing to the exact centre of the handle at the top, and a crease of the smaller circle pointing to the centre of the handle at the bottom, marks can be made on the top and bottom rims of the cups, coinciding with each crease (7). If lines are needed between the marks at the top and bottom a piece of sellotape can be stretched between the points and a line drawn down the edge (8). The same piece of sellotape can be used for each line drawn down the cup.

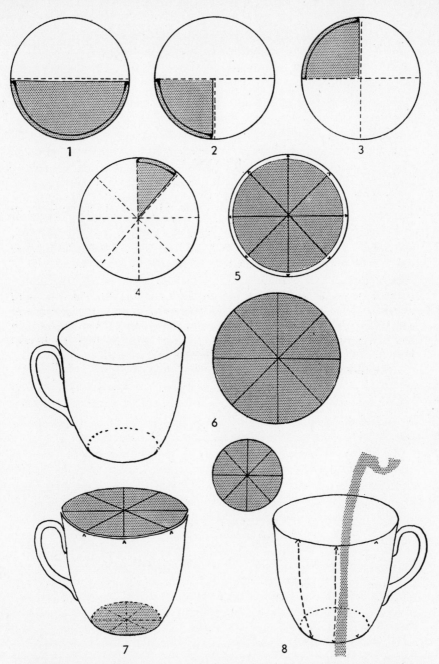

Diagrams showing the cut-paper method for dividing the surface of a plate or cup into equal parts. The method of working is described in Chapter 3.

PLATE I

1. *Tile.*

The shape in the background of this tile is in turquoise blue, to which a little raven black was added. The colour was applied with a pad. The superimposed line work is in black applied thinly, giving a grey effect. For the spotting, sky blue and ruby relief colours were used. The turquoise and black were on-glaze powder colours.

2. *Tile.*

Paris black in scribbled brush strokes was used for the dog motif in this tile. The white circles were scratched out while the colour was still tacky. The leaves surrounding the central motif were painted in free brush strokes in turquoise blue and the spotting in Paris black ; both colours were on-glaze powder colours.

The tiles were fired once.

PLATE I

4. BANDING

BANDS round the rims or bases of cups and bowls, and bands round saucer and plate edges, can be done quite expertly with some practice. By placing the little finger on the edge of the china, and using it as a guide for the brush held between the thumb and forefinger, and slowly turning the cup round with the left hand, a steady band of colour can be applied (page 22, 1).

Banding can also be done with the aid of a banding wheel, or one of the substitutes listed on page 9. It is essential that the article to be decorated should be placed exactly in the centre of the wheel, on which there are usually circles marked to assist in placing. However, when dealing with a plate whose edge is at an angle to the base, the placing is a difficult matter. It is helpful in this case to cut a collar, that is a strip of paper which is stiff enough to hold its position. The strip should be a little longer than the circumference of the plate and wider than the measurement from the rim to the surface of the banding wheel. This strip can be placed round the plate rim, the edges being held together with a piece of sellotape. In this way the size of the plate is transferred to the surface of the banding wheel, where the lower edge of the paper collar rests on it, and so greatly assists in centring the article (page 22). To prevent the plate slipping, it is a good plan to place a small piece of plasticine between the banding wheel and plate.

For banding a flat article, the wheel should stand on a stool or box lower than the height of the bench or work table. A piece of wood about $15'' \times 5'' \times \frac{1}{2}''$ sufficient for an arm-rest should be screwed to the bench, the wood projecting over the wheel, so that a brush can be held vertically over a plate. According to the breadth of band required a suitable brush should be chosen and be well charged with colour. Too little colour will not last the round of the plate, while too much will blob and blot. Practice alone will show the right consistency and quantity of the colour. This depends to some extent on the atmosphere. If it is found that the colour is drying too quickly, a few drops of oil of cloves will help to keep it moist. Oil of lavender also prevents over-quick drying, but is apt to make the colours spread. There are occasions when a slight spreading is used intentionally as a decorative effect.

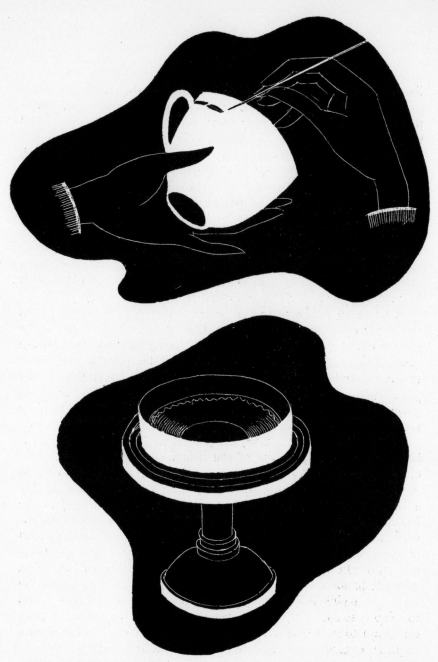

The method of banding a cup, using the little finger as a guide is shown in the top drawing. The drawing below shows the use of a paper collar to assist in centring a plate on the banding wheel.

Two positions of the hand. In the first, it is shown supported above the level of the wheel in the correct position for banding a plate. Below, the hand is shown in the position for banding a jar, bowl or cup.

23

The wheel is started spinning with the left hand. The right hand lowers the brush gently but firmly on the plate, until the revolving plate has caused a complete circle to be made. The brush should then be lifted very gradually to avoid a sudden darkening of colour at the join.

There are three types of banding.

1. *Clear banding.* One or more bands clearly defined, either the same colour and width, or varied colours and widths. Clear banding can be used as the only means of decoration, or in conjunction with other motifs.

2. *Spiral banding.* The effect of a spiral can be obtained by starting the wheel revolving at a good speed and placing the brush down in the centre of the plate ; as the plate revolves, the brush is drawn from the centre to the outer edge of the plate in a straight line, using the arm-rest as a straight edge. Because the plate is revolving the seemingly straight line will mark a spiral on the plate. This is difficult to do alone, but with one person revolving the wheel and one marking the line, there should be no difficulties.

3. *Diffuse banding.* Sometimes a few strong bands of colour are run on to a plate, and then with a slightly more liquid and different colour the lines are blended together in a spiral movement, in and out, from the centre to the edge. Very interesting colour effects can be gained by this method, but care should be taken not to overwork the colours, for too much mixing causes all the life and sparkle to disappear, making the results dull and muddy in appearance. Before using mixed colours see notes on test firing (page 27).

Motifs can be superimposed on a background of banding (frontispiece, 2 and 5). For this type of work the banding is done first and then fired or left to dry and harden. If the banding has not been fired, the superimposed motif must be done with a very sure hand since no alterations are possible without lifting the banding colours.

Cups are more difficult to manage on the banding wheel, because they have handles which seem very much in the way. With care it is possible to overcome this difficulty. The band should commence at the handle, and the cup revolved slowly enough to enable the brush to be lifted at the required moment.

Further use of the banding wheel is mentioned on page 27.

24

5. GROUND LAYING

It is sometimes an advantage if part or all of a piece of china be tinted or coloured. The method of doing this is called 'ground laying.' Some colours are better for ground laying than others. It is wise to make a test with a small amount of colour before grinding and mixing the full amount required for the work on hand. Blues, mauves and carmines are difficult to use and need more grounding oil than the yellow, green and red range. It would be well to avoid the usual tendency of beginners to use the colour too thick and too dry.

Oil, turpentine, flux and colours are used for ground laying in the same proportions as those given on page 12. A special grounding oil can be used with advantage in place of fat oil. A few drops of oil of cloves should be added to prevent the colour drying too quickly.

The method of stippling the colour on with a special stippling brush (brush at extreme right in drawing on page 8) results in an evenly speckled ground. The brush is used by dabbing the colour on in vertical dabs, the brush always striking directly on to the china without dragging from side to side. This method is often used as a border on the rims of plates, etc.

Another method of covering a ground is to use a pad. This should be made up preferably of lamb's-wool covered with a piece of silk. If there is any chance that the fluff from the wool might work through, two thicknesses of silk should be used. Cotton wool can be used instead of animal wool, but is inclined to be more absorbent, soak up the turpentine and leave the colour rather dry for working.

It is essential when laying a ground that the atmosphere should be as dust-proof as possible. It is inadvisable to work close to a fire, because there is always a certain amount of dust, and the heat is too drying. The china should be well cleaned with alcohol or methylated spirit. After the colour has been thoroughly ground, and the necessary oil added, it is a good plan to let it drip through a fine sieve. There are sieves specially made for this purpose, but two thicknesses of organdie muslin stretched over an egg cup, and held in place with a strong elastic band, serve the purpose quite well.

Some people prefer to work straight away with the pad, dabbing this lightly into the paint and transferring it to the china by dabbing in quick, light dabs until the area is covered, and then working with a light circular movement until the ground has flattened. Providing the ground is laid very thinly, a fair quantity of oil can be used, and this makes the work easier. If colour stronger than a mere tint is required, care must be taken, as too much oil in the mixture will craze when fired, or burn off in little blisters. If a dark ground is needed, this should be obtained by two or three applications, each being fired before the next is added.

Should the work become gritty or patchy it is waste of time to continue to dab with the pad. Better to add some more turpentine to the colour and disturb the surface by rubbing the pad over it in a circular motion. Once the whole surface is wet and ' movable ' the padding can be restarted. Quite often the second padding is successful where the first is not, as the surface has become slightly ' tacky ' and receives the colour more easily.

Some people find that laying colour on with a brush before padding is more satisfactory. For this a camel-hair brush with a flat point (page 8, centre) should be well filled with colour, and the surface covered in strokes laid side by side, never going over any part twice. The pad is then used with a quick, light circular movement, gently flattening and smoothing out the brush strokes. The pad should never be choked with colour, and should be wiped continually with a smooth clean rag. If the colour begins to lift, and patches of the white china show through, it indicates that it has been over-padded.

It is difficult to lay a ground over a large surface, as the part laid first is apt to dry before the whole surface is completed, thus making an invisible join of colour impossible. The best plan, when a large area is to be covered, is for two people to work at the same time.

When colouring the outside of a cup, the handle once more presents a problem. It is wise to have two pads ready, one very small and one a little larger. The colouring should be started at the handle and laid quickly from each side until the whole cup is covered ; the small pad should be used to flatten the colour round the handle, and the larger one for the rest of the surface.

A striped effect can be obtained on a cup, bowl or vase, by sticking bands of sellotape round the china and then padding colour over the surface. When the sellotape is removed, bands of white will be left on the coloured china. The edges of the bands sometimes need tidying up with the point of a knife once the colour is quite dry. These bands can be left plain, or be decorated with a simple design.

Sometimes a tint or colour is required inside a cup or basin, where it is impossible to use a pad. Quite an attractive ground can be laid with the help of the banding wheel. The cup must be centred and the banding wheel placed at the level described for banding a plate (page 23). A large flat camel-hair brush, well charged with colour, should be passed slowly and in a straight line from the centre to the rim of the revolving cup, up and down, until the complete surface is covered. There will be a slightly lined effect which adds character and interest to the work (Plate VI, 2).

Another method of tinting the inside of cups is to prepare colour in a fairly liquid condition and with a thick soft brush make a stroke across the rim from the inside outwards until the colour runs down inside the cup. This movement has to be repeated side by side, dipping the brush in the colour deposited at the bottom of the cup before each stroke. It may be necessary to go round the cup two or three times to get the colour evenly distributed. Surplus colour must be lifted out from the bottom of the cup with a dry, clean brush and then, after a few days when the sides are quite dry, the bottom can be scraped clean with a fine penknife. The removal of the deposit at the bottom of the cup is most important, as too much oil settles on the bottom and would not fire satisfactorily.

In spite of the large range of enamel colours, it is often necessary to mix colours. This can be done, but test firing should be made (pieces of broken china being kept for this purpose), as some colours fire more strongly than others, and some colours when mixed together cancel each other out, or in other words, eat each other up ; for example, ivory yellow mixed with carmine disappears when fired. Yellows often prove too strong for other colours, therefore when mixing colours with yellow, less should be used than would appear necessary in the palette.

Some reds, especially carmine, coral and poppy, fire down in the first firing and appear very faint. To achieve their full colour, three or four paintings may be necessary, each being fired before the next is applied. It is possible to lay a coloured ground, have it fired, lay a thin ground in another colour over the first, and fire for a second time. This method often gives a nice quality to a grounding, and is more interesting in colour than if the colours had been mixed together on the palette, applied and fired in one firing.

When mixing colours for grounding, or decorating sets of china, sufficient colour should be prepared to complete the whole set, as it is very difficult to match a grounding exactly. When tests are made, careful notes should be taken of the proportion of colours, flux and mediums used. Few people possess fine and accurate weighing scales for weighing small quantities, but a small spoon always measured level can give fairly accurate results. Thus, an imaginary note of quantities might be as follows :

      2 spoonfuls navy-blue powder colour.
      1 spoonful Paris black powder colour.
      1 spoonful flux.
      2 spoonfuls turpentine.
      $\frac{1}{2}$ spoonful fat oil of turpentine.
      5 drops oil of cloves.

PLATE II

PLATE II

All these circular dishes were given a single firing except example No. 1 which was fired twice, and example No. 6, which was fired three times.

1. Iridescent lustre was used for the background. It was applied with a flat camel-hair brush. The dish was then fired. Fine-line work in Paris black on-glaze powder colour, and spots in sky blue relief colour were added, and the dish refired.

2. The grounding was done in ground laying green (tube colour), and was applied with a pad. The design was scratched out with a metal point, after the ground had dried.

3. A tonal effect. Paris black on-glaze powder colour was scumbled on with a brush. The design was arrived at by removing colour, while it was still wet, with pieces of cloth, wooden and rubber implements. The dark accents were added with strokes of a brush.

4. The central shape was done in asphalt brown, No. 3 tube colour, the colour being removed to form the light spots. The filigree work was done with a pen in bright gold.

5. The design was done in superior blue, black, and lemon-yellow all on-glaze powder colours, applied with camel-hair brushes of different sizes.

6. A floral motif in direct brush strokes, after the style of peasant work. The colours used were : deep green and poppy red tube colours. Amber yellow, cobalt blue, and raven black, all on-glaze powder colours. This example was fired three times, the poppy red being freshly applied before each firing. (See page 28, paragraph 1.)

These motifs are used as stencils for the designs shown opposite.

6. TRANSFERRING AND STENCILLING

WHEN a large number of pieces of china are to be decorated with the same motif, or when a copy of any piece is required, it is useful to know how to transfer a design on to china.

In the case of designing and decorating a large number of pieces, such as a dinner or tea service, it is a good plan to obtain an odd plate, or cup and saucer, as like as possible to the set to be decorated, and to use this as a test piece. Considerable time should be spent on this sample, so that the best possible arrangement of line, mass and motifs can be arrived at. When completely satisfied with the appearance of the test piece, and when it has been fired to make sure the colours fire satisfactorily, a piece of transparent tracing paper should be placed round the design of, say, a cup; it should be joined with strips of sellotape at the handle. Pieces of plasticine over the rim will hold the paper in position and enable a careful tracing to be made of the main lines of the design. Very fine detail should not be traced, but added freehand, which will help to ensure that the work looks spontaneous and hand done.

When the tracing is complete, remove the tracing paper from the sample cup and, with a piece of carbon-paper between it and

30

Stencilled shapes can look hard and mechanical; sometimes the addition of a few brush strokes can counteract this tendency. The stencilled shapes above are indicated by the use of a printer's stipple. The designs are completed with free brush strokes. Sometimes a stencil, instead of being used to give a solid mass of colour, can be used as a guide for a design in outline. This method is illustrated by the fish motif in the top right-hand corner of the page.

the first cup to be decorated, fix the tracing paper in exactly the same position as it had been on the sample cup. If care is taken that the edges of the tracing paper follow the edges of the cup handle, there should be no difficulty. Proceed by drawing over the traced lines with a hard sharp pencil. If possible, make your tracing just outside the exact line, so that when painting the design it will not be necessary to pass the brush over the carbon line ; in this way a messy appearance is avoided, for all carbon lines will disappear in the firing.

Another method of reproducing a design many times is to use a stencil. Stencils can give a very unpleasant, hard design, but used intelligently and in conjunction with free brush work they can be quite satisfactory.

If the stencil is going to be used a great number of times metal stencil sheeting is advisable ; this is like a lead foil, which will wrap round curved surfaces and stand a great deal of wear. For most purposes ordinary stencil paper can be used, although if used very often the turpentine soaks in and the edges become flabby and frayed.

The design should be drawn or traced on to the stencil paper, then with the paper spread on a piece of glass the shapes cut out with a sharp stencil knife. The cut shapes should appear a fraction larger on the stencil than will be required on the finished article, to counteract the tendency for shapes to become smaller when stencilled, due to the thickness of the stencil.

The stencil can be held in position on the prepared china by means of plasticine or sellotape. A pad or a stipple brush should be used to push the colour through the stencil. If the edges are not quite clean when the stencil is lifted, the work should be left to dry and then the edges cleaned up with the pointed blade of a penknife. The work is then ready for the free brush strokes to be added, and these, if well done, can transform a somewhat mechanical design into one of freedom and fancy (pages 31 and 45). Stencil motifs can be superimposed one over the other, and in this way quite intricate designs can evolve.

7. FIRING

MENTION has already been made of ' firing,' and a little general information on this subject is necessary.

When colours are painted on the china, the design will be on the surface and will rub or scratch off, and is not permanent. The firing process fuses the colours into the glaze with which the china has been coated before leaving the pottery. On-glaze colours fire, or fuse, at approximately 750° to 800° centigrade. The colours vary in their firing properties, the reds usually requiring a greater heat than other colours. Unfortunately few people possess a kiln of their own, and must entrust their work to someone else to fire.[1]

The china is fired in a muffle kiln, which can be built to heat by means of solid fuel, paraffin, gas, or electricity. When the decorated china is put into the kiln the heat should be put on gradually so that the china expands slowly. The clammings should be left open for about half an hour, to allow fumes from the oils and essences used in mixing the colours to escape. The muffle should then be closed and the heat increased until the required temperature is obtained. Cones can be purchased for testing temperatures from approximately 600° to 2000° C. Once the heat has been turned off, care must be taken that the cooling is very gradual and the china left in the kiln until it is quite cool, otherwise a quick contraction will set in, and cracks and breakages will result.

8. GOLD AND SILVER

THE use of gold and silver is very popular with china decorators and can, if used with discretion, bring wealth and sparkle to the work. It is as well to remember that gold and silver ill-considered can be as unpleasant as an over-bejewelled woman. The beginner is apt to think only in terms of gold rims and handles. While this may be a very desirable way of using gold, it is not the only way, and sometimes the less obvious placing gives a more intriguing and exclusive finish.

Liquid bright gold and bright silver can be obtained in trial-size phials, and while they appear expensive, a small quantity goes a long way. The phials are very small, and it is a good plan to stand them in a nest of plasticine to prevent them being knocked over.

[1] Kilns are available at most Schools of Art. See also page 11, last paragraph.

C

Gold and silver are very easy to use, in fact, far easier than the colours. The liquid should be very well stirred. While the makers advocate that a little should be poured on to a palette, this method proves rather wasteful and amateurs usually prefer to use it straight from the phial. It should be applied to the china with a camel-hair brush, or, if very fine lines are needed, with a pen. Rather than risk too thick an application, it is safer to apply two thin coats. This would, of course, mean two firings.

It is very important that the edges of gold work should be clean and not smudged. If alterations are made, the lines to be altered and the surrounding area should be thoroughly cleaned. This is best done by moistening a piece of cloth with saliva and rubbing the china well. Marks not visible before firing often result in nasty mauve smudges after the firing process. Sometimes very faint marks on a fired article can be removed by rubbing carefully with some abrasive cleaner or a small touch of strong bleach. But prevention is better than cure.

If the liquid gold or silver becomes too thick, an essence made especially for thinning can be purchased. This essence is also good for cleaning brushes after gold has been used. If possible, brushes should be kept especially for the use with gold. If this is not possible, very great care should be taken that the brushes are absolutely clean.

Gold which is painted over another colour will fire matt. Sometimes a matt gold effect can be used to add variety to a design. The Chinese have made good use of matt and bright gold in their designs. Quite often a black edge with filigree design in dull gold is used as a border, leading the eye gently to touches of bright gold incorporated in the rest of the design.

China which is decorated with colours and gilding should, when possible, have the colours fired first, refiring after the gold has been applied. Certain reds need greater heat than the gold, and if used in the same design, a satisfactory firing for the colours may mean an overfiring for the gold, which then takes on a milky opaque appearance.

Gold can be obtained in powder form, but as this needs grinding and mixing, and burnishing with several different burnishers after firing, amateurs usually find the bright gold more convenient.

34

9. LUSTRES AND RELIEF COLOURS

THERE is a range of liquid lustres on the market. These, like the gold and silver, are applied with soft camel-hair brushes. The iridescent lustre gives a mother-of-pearl effect. It is easy to apply and less likely to go streaky than some of the coloured lustres. All should be well stirred and applied thinly. To obtain a really good lustre, three or four coats are often needed, each being fired before the next is applied. The same essence should be used as for the gold and silver, and no turpentine or oils used.

The more practised may like to experiment with some of the relief colours. These require the same preparation as on-glaze colours, but are applied more thickly. The colour can be allowed to drop from the brush to form small raised dots. Small areas of these colours can best be applied by holding the brush in a fairly upright position and letting the colour flow slowly on to the china. An outline should be made round the part to be coloured, and filled in afterwards with small dots placed closely together. These dots link up and make a smooth filling. A number of relief colours are transparent when they are fired, and give a glass-like effect.

There are in many homes specimens of Chinese china-ware, and it can be noticed how often use is made of small areas of relief colour. Even the inexpensive pieces display a masterly handling of colour, brush work and the distribution of flat and raised motives. Some years ago the market became flooded with inexpensive tea sets, etc., from China and Japan, and the names of these countries began to be associated with the commonplace in china decoration ; but some of the very best specimens of the craft come from these countries, whose peoples have behind them a very long tradition of china decoration.

10. FLORAL DESIGNS

THE majority of beginners in this craft associate floral designs, and no others, with china decoration. This is a pity, as it leads beginners to attempt painting flowers, especially rosebuds. By dipping brushes in the pinkest pink possible, by twisting it about on the china, by adding a few dark smudges to represent shadows,

PLATE III

All these specimens were fired once.

1. *Cup and Saucer.*

Spiral covering worked on the banding wheel in turquoise blue on-glaze powder colour coloured the inside of the cup and saucer. The design on the outside of the cup is fine brush strokes of Paris black on-glaze powder colour ; the star motifs and handle decoration are in bright silver.

2. *Tile.*

The background shape was padded on, in Gordon green on-glaze powder colour. This was allowed to dry and harden. The head was then painted partly over the coloured shape, and partly over the white surface of the tile in the following on-glaze powder colours : chrome yellow, Indian red, Spanish black and glorious blue. The flesh colour was a mixture of chrome yellow, with a touch of Indian red and black.

3. *Plate.*

The free brush-stroke design on the plate was done in cobalt blue on-glaze powder colour. Groups of lines and spots were used to give variety of textures.

4. *Mug.*

The motif used on the mug was made by dabbing a brush point on to the china firmly enough to cause the hairs to divide and form radiating lines. The motifs and rough stipple on the handle and base were done in Paris black. Spots of colour were removed round the base and on the handle, and filled in with bright gold.

5. *Bowl.*

A ground of Indian red was padded on to the inside of the bowl and then simple line motifs were scratched out with a sharp wooden point. The outside is spotted with crosses and circles in Paris black. Both colours are on-glaze powder colours.

6. *Plate.*

The border and centre of the plate are brush stippled in egg yellow on-glaze powder colour. The banding and line work are in purple-brown on-glaze powder colour.

PLATE III

PLATE IV

1

2

3

4

5

6

PLATE IV

1. *Coffee cup and saucer.*

The saucer has a broad border of bright gold, applied with a camel-hair brush. The filigree design on saucer and outside of the cup is in bright gold, applied with a pen. Salmon-pink on-glaze powder colour was applied to the inside of the cup, in the method described on page 27.

2. *Small plate.*

The grounding on this plate was done on the banding wheel in rubis d'or on-glaze powder colour. This was allowed to dry and harden before the design was scratched out with the point of a penknife.

3. *Oblong dish.*

Purple-brown on-glaze powder colour was applied to the inside of this dish with a pad. The line design was scratched out with a wooden point. Spots of brown were removed, and filled in with blue-bottle blue, tube colour. The outside of the dish has a striped design in dark brown.

4. *Mug.*

Alternate circles in deep green, and jonquil yellow, tube colours, were padded on to the mug. The simple flower shapes were scraped out. The leaves and stems are in Indian red, on-glaze powder colour, star motifs and lettering were of the same green.

5. *Bowl.*

The inside of this bowl was coloured with turquoise blue, on-glaze powder colour, on the banding wheel. The design was scratched out and spots of chamois tube colour were used to decorate the base. The same colour, in flowing lines, is used on the outside of the bowl.

6. *Tile.*

The method employed for this monochrome tile is described on page 41.

and a few crude green leaves, some very unlovely and commonplace designs are born.

Flowers and foliage have been, are, and can be used very charmingly ; and, providing the beginner is content to start with one of the more simple conventional treatments, the ability to use flowers, and at the same time not lose sight of design, and the relation of design to the shape of the china, will develop naturally.

It is helpful and often prevents vulgarity to decide on a scheme of colour and to work within that scheme. Thus it may be decided to work, say, in turquoise, gold and brown. If the design is to be of rosebuds and leaves, it is likely that the result will be more distinctive than if mere pink and green were used. It may be argued that nature is never wrong, and that pink roses and green leaves are beautiful, and so they are, but in how many lights do they appear really pink and green ? Because they are right in nature's settings, it does not necessarily follow that they are right when depicted on a man-made piece of china. Certainly it is good to be inspired by nature ; but designers have been given the power of selection and should make good use of it.

It is important when borrowing from nature to borrow nature at its best—the beautiful simplicity of a petal or leaf shape, and the easy flow of one stem from another. In an effort to be ' artistic,' some beginners feel it necessary to twist and distort nature in order to produce a design. The drawings on page 13 demonstrate the easy flow of line, and in some cases suggest a natural growth, such as could be a basis for floral pattern.

Direct brush strokes can be made to represent flower petals and leaves, and this is a good method to use in the early stages, for its results are often fresh and attractive. The peasant form of decoration makes good use of this method. However, great care should be taken not to overdo the brush-stroke work, as it can look over-slick and slippery. From time to time china appears in shop windows, labelled ' hand painted ' and often depicting large red poppies, combined with bright green leaves, growing out of the side of the plate. Each motif is done in fat brush-strokes, and the whole effect is very cheap and commonplace.

On Plate II are samples of various treatments. No. 6 shows the use of direct brush strokes to form flowers and leaves. A slight tonal effect can be obtained by allowing the colour to fall towards one end of a leaf or petal. Tone can also be suggested by painting

A few very simple floral and leaf motifs. However intricate the detail, a design is more likely to be successful if the construction of the forms is simple and straighforward. Forms which are twisted and contorted usually give a heavy, tired effect.

Slightly more intricate floral forms. Some of the flowers can be
easily recognized, and yet the aim has been towards simplicity of
growth and form.

a flower in flat colour and when dry adding another stroke of the same colour wherever a darker shade is required.

An attractive way of making floral designs is to paint the flowers and leaves in flat colours, according to a desired colour scheme, and then adding stems and outlining the flowers and leaves in a fine dark line. The lines can be done with a pen. As a precaution against blobbing, the pen should be tested on an odd piece of china after each dip into the colour, and the nib should be wiped continually with a non-fluffy rag.

The plate facing page 44 has its design based on the traditional rosebud. The roses are in orange-pink, the leaves grey-green, and the sprays are in brown. A broad band of blue, done on the banding wheel, leads out to a band of bright yellow. The aim has been towards a certain weight and wealth of colour.

There are occasions when a strong tonal effect is required in order to make a design ' stand out.' The tile on Plate IV shows one method of achieving this. In this case a ground—a mixture of black and a little red—was laid, and while the colour was still wet, the floral design was scraped out. Pieces of cloth and wood and tools made from rubber were used.

When a tinted background is wanted behind a floral design, the ground can either be laid and fired before the design is painted, or, if the designer has a very sure touch, it can be painted without firing, provided the ground colour is allowed time to dry and harden. It should be remembered that colours painted on a ground colour will, when fired, be affected by that colour, since, to some extent, they will fuse together—thus, blue painted over a yellow ground will tend towards green. Painting on an under-colour often gives a pleasant unity, but may tend towards dullness. This can be avoided if parts of the design have the background scraped away before being painted. If the ground colour is to be fired before the work is completed, it must be remembered that the desired shapes should be scraped away before firing.

11. NOTES ON DESIGN

THESE more or less technical notes have been punctuated with sentences on design. But it is in no way the intention to imply that design is of secondary importance to technical skill. A technically perfect piece of work, if it lacks inspiration, and is badly designed, will be less satisfactory to anyone of sensibility than an inspired and good design imperfectly executed. The latter may at least be distinctive while the former is likely to be commonplace. The aim, of course, should be towards a high standard in both design and craftsmanship.

A few points about design which may be stressed are : the advantage of working as directly as possible on to the china ; arranging the design to accentuate the salient features of the china ; emphasis on the individual character of a design rather than the imitation of a mass-produced design ; freedom of line, and, in connection with floral motifs, freedom of growth.

A small motif spotted over all, or part, of a piece of china can form an attractive design. This method of designing can demonstrate how important it is to work directly on the china. Assume, for example, that a jug has been chosen as suitable for decoration with a spot design. If a paper and pencil is used to map out the spotting, and it is planned on the flat, the result will be as shown opposite. To relate the size of motif and spacing to the jug, it is a good plan to sketch in the design roughly on the jug itself, and then, if the motif is to be a fairly elaborate one, a rough tracing can be taken from the jug. This tracing is then pinned to a drawing-board so that a careful drawing can be made in readiness for transferring, once all the trial lines and marks have been removed from the jug.

Counterchange is a form of design planned so that a light design appears on a dark background, alternating with the same design reversed in tone, to dark on light. This form of design looks well on borders, or used over complete surfaces (page 46).

The decoration of tiles offers great scope to the designer. Unlike jugs, cups and bowls, a tile has a flat surface, and is easy to work

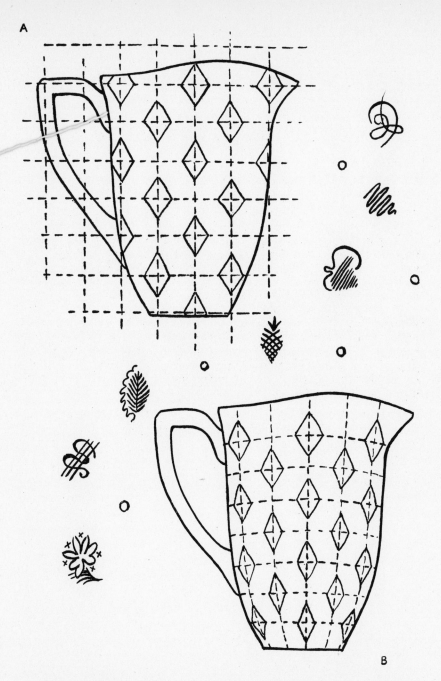

A

B

The jugs illustrated above show how a design drawn to measurement on a piece of paper and traced on to china has no relation to the shape (diagram A). The second diagram shows guiding lines indicated by dotted lines on the jug in character with its shape, and the diamond spot altered very slightly to suit the tapering of the jug at the base.

PLATE V

The design in the centre of the plate at the top of the page is based on the traditional rosebud : the bordering bands of colour were done on the banding wheel. For the dark band a mixture of blue-bottle blue and black tube colours was used. This colour was applied and fired four times in order to obtain the required depth of colour.

Flat floral decoration in pastel colouring covers a large portion of the lower plate. It has a light border composed of groups of crossed lines. The leaf shape on the small dish on the left is in Indian red with black lines superimposed and surrounding it. The smaller motifs are in dark brown and the spots in turquoise-blue relief colour. The dish on the right has a yellow and grey-blue border with a pee-brush stroke design in the centre in yellow.

44

PLATE V

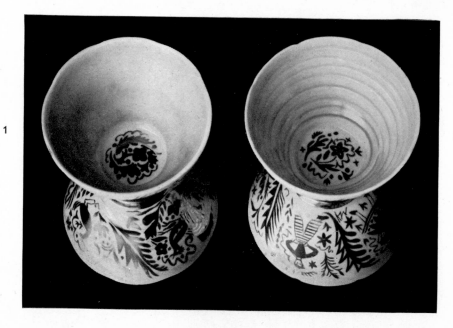

PLATE VI

1. *Small bowl.*

The design on the outside of this small bowl depicts birds, and foliage in bright silver. The inside has a turquoise-blue spiral filling done on the banding wheel. Photographed standing on a piece of mirror to show the under plan.

2. *Small bowl.*

The design on the outside depicts figures and foliage. The inside has a grounding of salmon-pink.

A lineal motif is sometimes rendered more interesting if it is super-imposed over a shape in a contrasting tone or colour. A few motifs are shown above illustrating this point.

The tile reproduced on Plate I has a blue-grey shape behind the figure which is in a fine grey line.

Simple or elaborate designs can be arrived at through the use of counterchange and can often be successfully used in china decoration. Above are a few simple diagrams showing this form of design.

on. The subject-matter, too, is less restricted than in the decoration of table ware. Tiles can be decorated boldly or in fine detail. They can be abstract in design, or tend to the naturalistic, depending on the purpose for which they are to be used. Sometimes tiles are framed and used as wall decorations ; sometimes they are set singly or in groups into fire-places. A large fire-place in a large room will probably take a boldly designed tile, while a small room with a delicately coloured smooth-tiled fire-place will look well with decorative tiles, finely designed and detailed, which may be enjoyed when seen at close range.

Some of the illustrations in this book have been included in the hope that they may add to its interest, not as designs to be laboriously copied, or to suggest that there is only one approach to design for this craft.

A text book is written to help those less experienced than its author. It is hoped for the reader that with growing technical proficiency, sense of design, and understanding of the scope and limitations of the craft, will come the feeling of freedom and delight in ' doing ' ; and also the realisation that text-book rules are made to be broken. The breaking of rules by the inefficient can lead to bad results, but a good craftsman and designer can ignore them in achieving individualism and originality.